For Christ's Sake

by
Dr. Jack Schaap

CREDITS
Project Manager: Dr. Bob Marshall
Assistant: Rochelle Chalifoux
Transcription: Martha Gilbert
Page Design and Layout: Linda Stubblefield
Proofreading: Kelly Cervantes, Rena Fish, and Maria Sarver

To order additional books by Dr. Jack Hyles,
please contact:
HYLES PUBLICATIONS
523 Sibley Street
Hammond, Indiana 46320
(219) 932-0711
www.hylespublications.com
e-mail: info@hylespublications.com

For Christ's Sake

"*Therefore if any man be in Christ, he is a new creature: old things are passed away; behold, all things are become new. And all things are of God, who hath reconciled us to himself by Jesus Christ, and hath given to us the ministry of reconciliation; To wit, that God was in Christ, reconciling the world unto himself, not imputing their trespasses unto them; and hath committed unto us the word of reconciliation. Now then we are ambassadors for Christ, as though God did beseech you by us: we pray you in Christ's stead, be ye reconciled to God. For he hath made him to be sin for us, who knew no sin; that we might be made the righteousness of God in him.*" (II Corinthians 5:17-21) To me, these are five of the most beautiful verses in the Bible.

Another equally beautiful verse is Ephesians 4:32. Probably most of us learned this Scripture as children. "*And be ye kind one to another, tenderhearted, forgiving one another, even as God for Christ's sake hath forgiven you.*" If you don't know this verse, you should commit it to memory.

This booklet is the result of an unbelievable counseling appointment. A man (whom I will call Bill, though that is not his name) came to me and said, "Brother Schaap, I'd like to ask a favor of my pastor. A man I love with all my heart has wronged some loved ones of mine, and in so doing, he has wronged me. He wronged me as much as an individual could ever wrong another man."

He told me the story, and as he told it, I felt my temperature rise. A flush came to my face, and I exhibited a righteous eagerness to avenge this man of the terrible wound that had been rendered to him. I found myself using angry words and harsh statements in trying to defend my brother who had been wronged and helping him to vent vicariously through my words.

As I spoke with Bill, I just knew he was going to say to me, "Can I take him to court? Can I hire a lawyer? Do you know one?"

This situation did not involve finances, but the wrongdoer had committed a very egregious error. I assumed he was coming to me for advice on how he could right a wrong legally, or morally, or Scripturally, or spiritually, or how far could he go within the confines of Christian grace without violating the Scriptures. I will be frank: I wanted to join with him. I wanted to pick up a weapon and bludgeon this enemy that had once been a so-called friend. I was angry for my brother in Christ; I was angry for my church member.

However, the words out of his mouth surprised me, convicted me, and humbled me greatly. This godly man said, "As wrong as this man has been toward me and my loved ones, what I want from you, Pastor, is advice on how I can reconcile the relationship."

"Quite frankly, I'm not sure I understand," I said. "Why would you want to do something like that? How about a bullet in the head?"

Bill looked at me and said, "I appreciate your helping me vent."

"I appreciate that because I'm angry for you," I acknowledged. "Let's talk about it. Are you really serious about reconciliation?"

He said, "Yes, Pastor. I really don't want to spend my life being hurt and angry. I don't think Jesus Christ wants me to do what you and I as men would want to do."

Bill's godly attitude launched us into a lengthy discussion

about how to reconcile with a man who did not deserve it—a man who I thought should be punished to the full extent of the law! As a matter of fact, this man should be punished and would be punished, except this godly church member had a dose of Christianity that was beyond most of our levels of Christianity.

"If you are truly serious about reconciliation," I proceeded, "you are talking about some very heavy doctrinal understanding."

"What do you mean?"

"Well, let me explain," I offered. "This whole matter of reconciliation is an extremely God-centered concept. The reason why we don't have reconciliation in the world today is that very few people understand the wisdom of how God established the procedure of reconciliation."

"I don't follow you," Bill puzzled.

"Please let me take it point by point with you," I urged. "Let's use God as the example of the One Who was wronged and leave you out of the equation for a while."

- God was wronged like no human being has ever been wronged. God was wronged like a child is wronged by a pedophile.
- God was wronged like a man whose wife leaves him for another man.
- God was wronged like Jeffrey Dahmer's victims were wronged when he killed them and then refrigerated their body parts so he could eat them later.
- God was wronged by mankind like John Wayne Gacy's victims were wronged when he murdered those 30-some boys and hid them underneath the basement of his house.
- God was wronged like Richard Speck wronged those nurses in Chicago when he crept into their room and murdered them with a bloodthirsty lust.
- God was wronged like Adolf Hitler wronged six million Jews.

- God was wronged like Joseph Stalin wronged 30 million Russians.
- God was wronged like Mao Tse-tung wronged 50 million Chinese Christians.

"These examples are merely light shadows compared to how God was wronged! God was wronged like all the wrongs that have ever been committed against everyone combined, and the Garden of Eden is the cause of all those wrongs. All the hurt that you feel, all the ambivalence that I have toward this person because of my love and respect for you, all the hurt that a child has who has been wounded by an abusive sexual predator is barely a minuscule drop in a bucket to the wrong God has had done to Him by all of mankind. Our sin in the Garden of Eden caused all of these wrongs and was the causal factor for all of the wrongs of mankind against God for all the ages. The hurt from every wrong you can think of was felt by God."

"But," I added, "let's delve deeper. To add insult to injury, it wasn't as though we acknowledged our wrong and rushed back to God and said, 'We apologize!' No! We added insult to the injury for all of these millennia because we have haughtily said, 'We will **not** confess our wrongdoing! We do not agree with You! Would You get off of our case? Would You get out of our lives? We would rather bow down to a hunk of gold or a piece of wood! We would rather deny Your existence! Would You please get out of my face?!' "

As I was explaining about the way mankind has wronged God to this good man who had been wronged, big tears welled up in his eyes. Bill said, "I don't know that I can totally understand, but I feel for God."

I continued, "We replace God with anything from a cow, to the sun, or even a plastic statue that sits on the top of the dashboard of our car. We supplant Him with everything from paper money to gold coins, and even to making absurd statements like,

'There is no God!' Mankind has even denied that He exists."

"Not only did God get wronged by us," I reinforced, "the average man and woman is so ignorant of what we did to God that we almost thumb our nose at God and say, 'Why would I admit I'm wrong?' "

"On top of that, the common statement made by many when anything bad happens is, 'Where was God when this happened?' Instead, we should be saying, 'Where were we when the sin of the Garden of Eden was corrupting everything?' Why have we done insult to God? What nerve do we have to say to a holy God, 'Why do You let bad things happen to us?' I have no doubt that God wants to retort, 'Don't you dare shake your fist at Me!!' "

Bill listened intently in the office that day. I could tell that he was moved by the thought that God's hurt was even deeper than the injuries he was personally experiencing. He saw, perhaps for the first time, just how wrong it was to question God.

Questioning God

Too many Christians tend to cross-examine God when so-called bad enters their life.

- "Why did my loved one pass away?"
- "Why has cancer entered my body?"
- "Why do I constantly fight sickness?"
- "Why do I always lose?"
- "Why was I overlooked for the varsity squad again?"
- "Why wasn't my daughter chosen for a cheerleader?"

In answer to these questions and others like them, God says, "How dare you question Me! Why don't I ask you, 'Why don't you bow the knee to Me?' Why don't I ask you, 'What right do you have to breathe My air and to spout blasphemies out of your mouth? What right do you have to insult Me?' What right do you, the created one, have to say to the Creator, 'What are You doing?' I can do anything I want to! I made you!" Instead, we continually insult Him, and God says, "Why would you wonder that I'm angry?"

After we have incessantly insulted God with our petty, offended attitudes, God becomes extremely angry. I don't want to burst anyone's bubble about his concept of God, but I want everyone to have a solid, scriptural understanding of what God feels like. God is angry!

"I Thought God Loved Us!"

I will address the subject of God's love later. First, we must realize that God is angry. He is so angry with man that He said, "I am going to kill you! No, I believe I will kill you twice! I will give you a body that will age, die, and return to dust. Then, I will kill you again!" God was extremely angry with man and said, "I will kill you for defiling this world. I will kill you for crippling what I have given you. I will kill you and destroy you."

"I Thought Sin Brought God's Judgment!"

Who do you think brought that sin penalty to all mankind? God designed the plan, and He gave Adam ample warning. *"And the LORD God commanded the man, saying, Of every tree of the garden thou mayest freely eat: But of the tree of the knowledge of good and evil, thou shalt not eat of it: for in the day that thou eatest thereof thou shalt surely die."* (Genesis 2:16, 17) When Adam ate the fruit, God said, "You are going to die, Adam!" Over 900 years later, that man died! If Adam hadn't been born again, he would have died the second death!

God said to mankind, "Not only will I kill you twice, I'll kill you for eternity! Every day of your life for a timeless existence, you will die! Every day you will be reminded of the fool you played! Every day you will be reminded of the hatred I have for your sin!

Every day in eternity you will cry out for mercy, and I will say, 'Shut up! I never knew you!' "

My Bible says that the day will come when, in flaming fire, He will take vengeance on them who knew Him not! *"In flaming fire taking vengeance on them that know not God, and that obey not the gospel of our Lord Jesus Christ: Who shall be punished with everlasting destruction from the presence of the Lord, and from the glory of his power."* (II Thessalonians 1:8, 9) The Bible says that the unsaved will be punished with everlasting destruction in a place away from the presence and the power of the Lord.

Why would He punish His creation with such a wrathful vengeance? Because, quite simply, His creation chose not to obey the Gospel of our Lord Jesus Christ.

God said, "Everything that I am, you won't have because you don't want Me! I am Light! You would rather live in darkness. I am Life! You would rather have death! I am Peace! Since you would rather not have the peace I have to offer, I will give you torment! I am Rest. Since you would rather not have the rest I have to offer, I'll give you pain. I am Love, but you would rather have strife, anger, contention, murders, revelings, and hatred. You will suffer strife and war! Go ahead and kill each other! You are just going to die again and again and every day thereafter for a timeless eternity. Go ahead and thumb your nose at God and say, 'You can't kill me!' and I'll kill you every day in eternity!"

God can take life, and He can give life! I once read about a suicide where a man wrote in the note he left behind, "God will not win!" Unless that man was saved before he pulled the trigger, he is finding out every moment that God won!

No Love in Hell

Let me say this: People who die and go to Hell are not loved in Hell! There are no loudspeakers in Hell blasting a message from Satan that says, "I love you. I'm sorry you're in Hell." NO! If there are loudspeakers in Hell, the message that thunders forth and crashes and echoes off the walls of the bottomless pit is, "Damned! Cursed! Hatred! Vengeance! Murder! Blood! Damned! Cursed! Hatred!" The ones who reside there hear that message again and again and again for all time! They are constantly reminded that God was angered every time they said, "Don't tell me what to do!"

- *"...Vengeance is mine; I will repay, saith the Lord."* (Romans 12:19)
- *"Knowing therefore the terror of the Lord...."* (II Corinthians 5:11)
- *"In flaming fire taking vengeance on them that know not God...."* (II Thessalonians 1:8)

The Bible teaches that we have a wrathful God! I don't believe I can fully explain to you His wrath or the extent of His wrath! The Bible says, *"Then shall he say also unto them on the left hand, Depart from me...."* (Matthew 25:41) God thunders, "GET OUT FROM HERE! I NEVER KNEW YOU!"

Too late some will cry, "Lord, Lord!"

God will retort, "Don't call Me Lord!"

Some will plead, "But we have prophesied!"

God will hurl back, "Get out! Don't ever come back!" At that time God will simply be repaying mankind for all the wrong that has been done to Him.

A Bleak Future

If we were to stop the writing of this booklet at this point, the picture is very bleak indeed! Mankind has a big problem. Our omnipotent God is a complex God. While He is extremely angry, He is also love. For lack of a better illustration, let me explain it this way: a "tug-of-war" goes on inside of God. Inside the heart of God resides His holiness. God pronounces a judgment and says, "In flaming fire, vengeance is Mine; I will repay," and a still, small voice inside of Him whispers, "But I still love them."

Holiness says, "Be quiet! They have offended My holiness. They have wrecked and ruined everything I have created. They defiled My earth, they polluted My name, and they have marred My testimony!"

The still, small voice asks, "Don't You love them though?"

God's Holiness shoots back, "But I don't know how to bring them back because I can't take an injury that is any worse than that which I have already received."

Then God, in His incredible love, concedes, "I don't know how to get them back."

Holiness rejoins, "I don't want to get them back. I'm so angry at them! I'm going to kill them and send them to Hell."

The love of God says, "I agree with You, but what are You going to do about Your unfailing love?"

God's Holiness frustratingly answers, "I don't know! Perhaps I can force-feed them with My love and shove it down their hateful throats."

His Love asks, "But how will You accomplish that?"

His Holiness answers, "I don't know! I don't know how to say I love them! I'm too angry at them! I am too full of wrath!"

His Love replies, "I know, but what are We going to do about love? They are created in Your image."

His Holiness argues, "I know! Don't remind Me! I know they're in My image, and that's what really ticks Me off! I made them in My image, and they live like the Devil!"

Reconciliation— Such a Beautiful Word!

My mind returned to Bill and his struggle to reconcile with an individual who had offended in such a vile manner those he loved. I believe I could understand in a diminutive way the torture God must have felt over mankind as I listened to Bill saying, "I'd like to take this guy and just.... He has hurt my family so much. But it wouldn't be right! How do I reconcile this, Brother Schaap?"

I said, "The same way God did!"

"How did God do it?"

"Listen carefully to me," I replied. "God still loves us. While Christ was hanging on that cross, the love of God was stammering, 'Oh, love of God! How rich and pure.' " God cannot and He will not personally come to anyone and try to reconcile with him. The person who thinks God will someday come to him to negotiate a reconciliation has had a bad dream! God makes no personal house calls because if God saw you, He would kill you. He is that wrathful.

God says, "I will not go to an unsaved person who has defiled My creation, who has mocked My Holy Name, who has brought shame and reproach to everything holy, who has taken My image and made Me into a cow or nothing more than a gold coin, and who has made My created sun into something to bow down to and to kiss. In some cases, these unsaved ones have even selected a man, put a robe on him, and call him "Father." I alone am the Father! ["*And call no man your father upon the earth: for one is your Father, which is in heaven.*" (Matthew 23:9)] They even call each other by the name "Reverend." *Reverend* is a name reserved for Me! ["*He sent redemption unto his people: he hath commanded his covenant for ever: holy and reverend is his name.*" (Psalm 111:9)] Holy is the Lord."

"That is why God doesn't personally go soul winning. God absolutely does not want to work with mankind. He does not want to reconcile with those He created."

I further explained to Bill, "If you were to go to this man who injured you and say, 'You know that I know that you did wrong. All I want you to do is to agree with me that we both know you did wrong,' and that wrongdoer said, 'You're crazy!' you would probably want to...."

"Kill him!" Bill hastily interrupted.

"Right!" I agreed. "God can't risk being mocked because the Bible tells us that God is not mocked. God cannot allow anyone to do that to Him again. He says, 'You "took" Me in the Garden of Eden once, but I'm no fool. After the next time we see each other, I will never have to see you again. The next time I see you, I will send you into outer darkness with the devils, and they will terrorize you for eternity. I never want to see you again!' "

Bill then asked, "So then how do I reconcile with this man who bludgeoned our friendship?"

"You reconcile with him," I answered, "the same way God does! That person needs to admit that he wronged you, but if he told you that he didn't agree with your assessment of the situation, it would wound you so much that I think it would push you over an edge of sane judgment. Then you would lash out in vengeance—acting like God."

"I think you might well be right," Bill said.

"What you really need is someone who loves you and who knows him—someone who has not been wounded like you have been and someone who cares about both of you—to help with the reconciliation," I advised. "You need someone who could go to him and say, 'You know what? I'm like you are; I do a lot of wrongs, and I'm really sorry for what happened in this particular situation. For all I know, it's my fault, but I know this person is a very good man, and I believe you two should get together and at least shake hands. It would mean the world to me if you would say you're sorry. That's all you need to do! Just say, 'I'm sorry!' Just tell him that he is right and you are wrong. That's all you have to do!' "

Bill replied, "If that man would just come to me and say, 'I'm wrong, and I'm sorry,' I'd have my hand out to grasp his in a heartbeat. I would say, 'That's all I wanted to hear.' I would love to hear that."

"That's all God wants, too," I said. "That's all God wants to hear! All God wants to hear is for man to say, 'God! I can't believe what I did! I don't know how You can even put up with me! You're right, and I'm wrong. I did wrong against You, and if You can find some place in that incredible heart of Yours to forgive me, it would be the greatest thrill in all the world to know that You don't hate me anymore. I just want to know! I want to know, God, are You willing to reconcile? Can we please negotiate?' "

Bill's expressed desire for reconciliation echoed the same dilemma faced by a Holy God. A mediator was needed—one to bridge the gap between **the perfect** and **the perverted**.

Only for Christ's Sake

God thunders out His answer with His words, "I'll forgive them—but only for Christ's sake."

Jesus goes to the Father, and He says, "Father, I have an idea, and I just want to know what You think about it."

"Jesus, I am open to any idea You have."

"I have this idea whereby I can negotiate a settlement of peace between You and man," Jesus explained. "I believe I can arrange a contractual agreement where man agrees—flatly and honestly—that You are right and he is wrong, and that he did the sinning and that You are holy. If I can get man to admit that He is wrong, God, all You have to do is give Me Your word because I know You'll keep Your Word. If I can arrange a reconciliation, then, not for man's sake, but for My sake, would You forgive man?"

God said, "I will!"

Did you know that God doesn't forgive you for **His** sake? Did you know that God doesn't forgive you for **your** sake? Did you know that the only reason God ever considered forgiving mankind is that the second member of the Godhead said, "I will put My life on the line! If I can't arrange a reconciliation, then send them to Hell; but if they agree they're wrong, would You forgive them?"

God answered, "Only for **Your** sake!"

Jesus said, "I'll make it happen!"

Allow me to share how bad it really got. Jesus left Heaven, and He came to earth, filled with the anticipation that He would be able to reconcile mankind to His Father. He just knew He could make it happen. After all, He's God! He can do anything. However, even as He came unto His own, His own said, "You have a devil!"

I have no doubt that all the feelings that God had been feeling welled up in Jesus Christ! He looked at ungrateful man and said, "I reject you! You will never, ever have a chance. I'll send you to Hell. It will be better for Tyre and Sidon than for you because you don't know Who I am!"

A few Gentile people said, "We do! We do!" A few unlearned Gentile people like a black man from Ethiopia; an itinerant fisherman from the Sea of Galilee; a cheating, lying tax collector; and a scoundrel named Zacchaeus said, "I know Who You are! Is that opportunity for reconciliation open for me?"

Jesus said, "As many as receive Me, to them I'll give the power to become the sons of God."

When Jesus went back to Heaven, the Father said, "Well? What happened? Did they accept Your proposal?"

Jesus replied, "It didn't go very well, Father."

The Father asked, "But were You able to negotiate a contract? Is there reconciliation?"

"Well, it's like this," Jesus ventured. "I went to the most promising people—those to whom You had given Your Word, those to whom we had sent the prophets, and those who knew the most about Us. They made fun of You. They put Me on a cross! They stripped Me naked. They blasphemed Your holy name! God, the Father, they are despicable creatures! Send them to Hell, Father!"

God the Father asked, "Is that it?"

Jesus replied, "No, all is not lost. There are some low-life, ignorant people who do not know what the Bible says. They lie, cheat, steal, murder, rape, pillage, fornicate, and commit all manner of sin! They are such a sinful people, but they want to sign the contract."

The Father said, "So the only ones who want to seek reconciliation with Me are losers—heathen, barbarians, Gentiles, and idol-worshippers. These kinds of people really want to sign a contract with the God of the universe?"

"Remember," Jesus said, "we discussed this reconciliation, and You made a statement that for **My** sake, You would forgive them."

God Almighty said, "I will keep My word because I am God!" *"In hope of eternal life, which God, that cannot lie, promised before the world began."* (Titus 1:2)

As Christians we should say, "Thank You, God! You cannot tell a lie!" We are saved because God doesn't lie!

God the Father looked at the Son and said, "Jesus, can You tell me how We are going to solve this situation? You were going to negotiate a reconciliation. Now what do You suggest?"

"I suggest that we mark a date on our calendar," Jesus said, "And on that date we burn the earth to ashes including every idol; every coin; every dollar bill; every temple; every human being: every grave; every crypt; and every blasphemous, ungodly, perverted, lying human being. Kill them! Burn them!"

The Father took out His pen, looked at His calendar for eternity, and said, "So ordered! The day of judgment is set! This earth will burn with fire!" *"But the day of the Lord will come as a thief in the night; in the which the heavens shall pass away with a great noise, and the elements shall melt with fervent heat, the earth also and the works that are therein shall be burned up."* (II Peter 3:10)

"But who," God asked, "is going to sign the contracts of those motley losers who want to broker a reconciliation?"

Jesus said, "I thought perhaps You would ask Me that question. Father, I hate to say it, but I think We need to contract it out because there isn't anyone who knows You who wants to soil his hands with sinful mankind."

Sign the Contract!

"To **whom** will You contract out this plan of reconciliation?"

Jesus answered, "The only people I know to contract it out to are the people who sign the contract. I suggest We group them together in units called local churches. My suggestion is that We have a contract with that local church and that We tell them they need to get busy and tell every human being to get saved or they will spend an eternity in Hell!"

The Father said, "Son, do You mean We are going to put all of Heaven and Hell in the hands of some losers and hope they catch the vision."

"Yes," Jesus replied.

God the Father asked, "Why?"

"Because when many of them say they are wrong, such an incredible fire lights up in their soul," Jesus explained. "They feel so clean and refreshed. They seem so forgiven, and like innocent little children again. Your power of forgiveness washes them white as snow and cleanses them of all their sin! It's like they have been born again!"

The Father said, "I like that plan!

"They're so happy, Father! You know I've never known sin, but for a few moments on the cross I felt it, and God, it's something You never want to feel. It's an indescribable pain, a dreadful terror You never want to know! But God, when You resurrected Me from the grave, I felt like those people do when they are born again!"

On God's Behalf

You and I, as a local church, have contracted with God as an outside firm to do the business of reconciliation. We visit a blinded, distorted, blasphemous, ungodly, filthy, perverted world, and we say, "I know what you're like, and I know Someone Who loves you. I am here on God's behalf to tell you that if you'll ever in your lifetime say, 'I'm sorry! I'm so sorry, God!' He'll do something inside of you that is indescribable. He'll write your name in the Book of Life. He'll make you a citizen of His celestial city. He'll become the Mayor and the King of your city. He will become your Father. You will live forever! Your sins are washed away! Your burdens are rolled off your back! Your heart will be cleansed. You will walk with a spring in your step, and His glory will show on your face! You will have forgiveness in your heart! Your name will be written down in Glory! It's great!"

Our job as a soul winner is to make reconciliation so good that every Hell-deserving object of the wrath of God says, "I want that!" If we don't tell them, no one else will. God is very angry at six billion, eight-hundred million souls! *"He that believeth on the Son hath everlasting life: and he that believeth not the Son shall not see life; but the wrath of God abideth on him."* (John 3:36) Nearly seven billion people will never hear the name of Jesus Christ if we don't tell them! God will not tell them, and neither will Jesus Christ.

Jesus negotiated the reconciliation, and He paid the price in full! On God's behalf, He signed His name, but not even Jesus will leave Glory anymore. The next time He comes, it will be in flaming fire to take vengeance. Therefore, if we as Christians do not tell those who are unsaved, they will automatically go to Hell!

Bill looked at me and said, "Brother Schaap, do you know **anyone** who could help me with this person who is my enemy?"

"You need a savior," I said. "You need a friend."

As Bill stood up to leave my office, I said, "My guess is that you and he will always be enemies."

~18~

Bill left my office that day still looking for a mediator and still looking for someone to make the effort of reconciliation seem appealing.

Tell the World!

On behalf of Jesus Christ Who called me to pastor First Baptist Church of Hammond, may I say, "If you don't tell the lost, then God will always be their enemy because God hurts so badly that He will not risk being hurt a second time."

I fall on my face in my prayer closet, and I say, "God, I'm so sorry."

God hears my prayer, and I believe He says, "Good! What are you doing about it?"

When I say, "God, I'm doing my very best," He replies, "It's not good enough!"

"But God, I believe I am trying as hard as I can."

I can almost hear His voice as God says, "Trying hard isn't good enough! How can 5,000 more people be enough? There are seven billion people in the world! Stop telling Me that you are doing your best! Find a way to tell the whole world that I am coming back, and I will not come to another cross. I will be coming with fire and damnation! Tell them!"

Christian, whom have you told the wonderful plan of reconciliation? Whom have you told that God will forgive them for Jesus' sake?

When an unsaved person refuses God's gift of eternal life, I immediately say, "I have a duty to warn you then. I am under contract by God Almighty Himself! I must warn you. You can reject the love of God through Christ Jesus. In so doing, you have sentenced yourself to eternal damnation!"

I spent about 45 minutes witnessing to a sharp, bright, college-aged young man. When I finished talking to him about the Gospel, I said, "I want to ask you something, my friend. I have given you a clear presentation of the Gospel according to God. Do you have any questions?"

"No, sir," he said. "You did a fine job explaining how I can go to Heaven."

"Thank you, but do you understand it?"

"Yes," he acknowledged, "I understand it."

"Will you bow your head and trust Christ as your Saviour?"

He asked, "Why?"

"I want you to bow your head out of respect for God," I explained. "I want you to repeat a prayer after me like I give when I marry a bride and a groom. I want you to humbly tell God that you are sorry."

"No," he adamantly replied.

"Then it is my duty to tell you that if you are rejecting Jesus Christ, you have sentenced yourself to Hell."

He asked, "I sentenced myself?"

"Yes, sir. You sentenced yourself to Hell."

"Go through it one more time then," he instructed.

Twenty minutes later I asked, "Do you still want to reject it?"

"No, sir," he maintained. "I may not agree with everything you believe, but I am surely not stupid."

"I want you to get off your chair and get on your knees."

"Anything you say, sir," he acquiesced.

When he got on his knees, I opened the Bible, and I said, "I want you to put your hand on the Holy Bible." He placed his right hand on the Bible and put his left hand over his heart. "God Almighty," He prayed, "You have a right to be angry at me, and I'm sorry." Then his voice caught because the emotion of what he was doing caught up with him. The tears welled up in his eyes, and they began to drip off of his face onto my Bible. "God, I don't want to go to Hell." I could feel his body shake as the emotion of what he had just said 20 minutes earlier began to hit him.

I don't want anyone to go to Hell! I know what it is like to be a sinner. I believe I can say that I understand how the songwriter C. Austin Miles felt when he penned the following words:

"I was once a sinner, but I came
Pardon to receive from my Lord:
This was freely given, and I found
That He always kept His word.

There's a new name written down in glory,
And it's mine, O yes, it's mine!
And the white-robed angels sing the story,
'A sinner has come home.'
For there's a new name written down in glory,
And it's mine, O yes, it's mine!
With my sins forgiven I am bound for heaven,
Nevermore to roam."

I know what it is like to be a sinner. I know what is it like to bow my head and receive forgiveness and the love of God. I know what it is like to lift my head and feel that incredible born-again experience—to be saved!

Have **You** Told Anyone?

I want the whole world to know it because there is no thrill or joy like knowing Jesus as your personal Saviour. If you and I don't tell the lost, then we didn't keep our part of the contract!

When I go to Heaven, I will meet God face to face because of Jesus. I will look at Jesus and I'll say, "I'm looking at You, Jesus. I'm here because of You!"

He will say, "Tell me when it happened! Did you bring anyone with you?"

Those I won to Christ will look at me and say, "Jesus, I'm here looking at Your face and Your Father's face because of him," and

I will be very, very happy that I kept my part of the contract.

Have you told anyone? Is there anyone born-again because of you? There are 7,999,999,999 more waiting to hear! Let's keep our part of the contract and go tell them. Let's help reach them as agents **for Christ's sake**!